HEALING

HEAL YOUR MIND
HEAL YOUR BODY
LOVE YOUR LIFE

2nd Edittion

By Angel Graff

Contents

Introduction

In this day and age, there is so much confusion. With everyone depending upon technology, people are confused about what it takes to make their lives fulfilled. Is it ownership of all the trimmings that make life enjoyable? Is it all about what you are and what you earn? Unfortunately, none of those things count for very much in the order of things because they are impermanent. These are merely props in our lives. They don't help us to have a better life. They merely give us toys to play with that may even be complicating our lives. People are up to their limits on credit cards and ready to throw in the towel because life is demanding too much of them. Why?

The answer lies in what you perceive as important in your life. Many of the ailments that people suffer today come as a direct result of not depending upon real relationships any more. Virtual ones are the answer to all your problems. What isn't talked about is how much damage human beings are doing to themselves and how they are forgetting values that may help them to help themselves to heal and to learn to love their lives. Your mind and your body depend upon you to use those traditional values of support that they need and yet, as a society, we are moving further and further away from the core values that keep us healthy and happy.

This book is written with you in mind. If you have ailments or if you are unhappy with what life is throwing at you, it's time to take a step off the roundabout and start to find grounded values that last longer than the latest iPhone. That's not what it's all about. So many people are turning to doctors and asking for help. Why? Because somewhere along the line they have lost their support system which is essential to emotional health as well as general health. Turning to pills instead of tackling the real issues is becoming a known phenomenon of the 21st century.

In 2012, statistics were gathered worldwide to find out how many people were being treated for depression. A staggering 121 Million people worldwide were known to be suffering and being treated for depression. That's got to tell you that something is very amiss in the world. When you look at the global spread of depression, it's interesting to note that third world countries are the lowest on the list. Does that make them better equipped to deal with depression or does that just mean that people don't have the money to go and seek medical help. Many are on the borderline starvation level and perhaps see mental health as a minor issue. What is obvious from these figures though is that mental health in developed countries is spreading and growing regardless of medications being available.

If you are sick of the commercial side of feeling well, perhaps it's time to look at more holistic ways of dealing with your health and welfare. Within your body and mind, you have more power over the way that you feel than you might imagine. This book tells you how to heal your mind and heal your body because both are part and parcel of the same equation.

Instead of turning to the nearest chemical medication to find happiness, it's time to take responsibility and learn that there is a spiritual side to everyone's nature that they can tap into at any time. It won't line the pockets of pharmaceutical companies but it will make for a happier world. Since 1988, prescriptions for anti-depressant medication had risen by 800 per cent and depression is on the rise. It may be a good time to step back and assess your life and to heal both your body and mind by other means.

Many of the drugs prescribed in this day and age have so many side effects that it's hard to tell whether it's the illness itself that is making the patient sicker or the drugs that they choose to take. While we would not recommend changing any regime that you are on without consultation with your doctor, we would advocate looking at your life from a totally different perspective because the healing power of the mind is amazing, and the healing power of the body is equally well developed. You just need to know how to tap into it in order to reap the benefits that will make your life a happier place to be.

Chapter 1 – Assessing Your Life

"Your pain is the breaking of the shell that encloses your understanding."

Kahlil Gibran

Read the quotation written above. From it you can learn a great deal about life and the pains that you suffer through your unhappiness or your illness. Kahlil Gibran is one of my favorite philosophers for a reason. This Lebanese born philosopher wrote a book called "The Prophet" and it wasn't until I read it that my own understanding of life was opened up and I was able to assess my life's worth. It's a very clever quotation and so true. When you feel pain, it is indeed the shell of your understanding being broken. Some decide that they want to find answers to that pain by traditional means that they have grown up with. For example, they may feel that their suffering needs to be treated by doctors. Others seek help through their Gods by praying for help. However, these are not the only avenues open to you and in fact often hide the true healing that is possible through more spiritual means.

The pain of heartbreak, the desperation of loss and the constant feeling of being incomplete are not things that can be treated with medication. Often prayers are said that seem to be unanswered, though there is a definite connection between healing and spirituality, as this book will show. It really doesn't matter what religion you are or what path you follow in your religious life. You may choose to ignore religion altogether, but you cannot deny that mankind needs some kind of healing when you look at the statistics and at the unhappy faces that you see every day of the week. Why, when life is so plentiful, are people less and less content with their lives? The answers may be easier to glean than you might imagine, but before you can actually put spiritual thought into practice, you need to strip back the barriers to actually appreciate what it is that you are working with.

That is the equivalent of what Kahlil Gibran cites as "breaking the shell" and there are ways that this works very well indeed and I relate from personal experience because it's the only way I know how to describe it. I am not qualified other than having experienced great sadness within my life, though through my searching for healing, what I found was astounding and it's available to anyone who seeks it, which is what prompted me to write this book.

From the moment that you wake in the morning to the moment you go to bed at night, life presents you with opportunity to enjoy the life that you have. Yet, the figures say that people are not finding that opportunity and that they are seeking ways to heal themselves because their lives are not giving them what they need. You need to strip back the veneer, get away from all the trappings of life and take a real voyage of discovery to find out who you are in the order of things. This, in turn, will help you to achieve a better understanding of your needs.

In my case, I chose a hill in the middle of the wild countryside as my haven. I chose to visit it at sunset when the world was at peace. Away from all modern gadgetry and staring into the beauty of the scenery that stood in front of me, I found something that perhaps was lacking from my life. I found humility. As you behold that stunning beauty, you begin to realize how small you are and that's a good thing, rather than a negative thing because it puts life into perspective. Looking over that sight where the hills meet the sky, the wonderment of life hit me hard at first. It was like a "wow" moment, and perhaps I hadn't experienced one of those since childhood. Suddenly, it wasn't about how much my bones hurt or about whether my back was giving me problems. It was about seeing all the positive things in their true colors. None of those small irritations of life were important any more. I knew I was small, but I also knew that I was part of this huge universe and that my part in it was every bit as important as anyone else's.

Humility helps you to break that shell that you hold around yourself when you become insular in your world. Choose somewhere awe inspiring to strip back the layers of unhappiness. Choose somewhere where you begin to believe in yourself because when you do, you will always have a safe harbor for those moments when life becomes too overwhelming. In this space, you can assess your life. Your problems in your everyday life seem so small in comparison with the beauty that you are presented with and this is the best environment on Earth to make decisions that are going to affect the rest of your life. In the chapters that follow, I will show you how to use that place to recharge your batteries, to make you feel whole and to help you to understand how nature helps the healing process.

Once you understand, you won't mind the pain of the eggshell breaking. It will be liberating because once you take on the responsibility of healing yourself through natural means, you really do take charge of your own happiness and that's vital to a great future that you can share with your loved ones, teaching them how to become happy in their lives too.

Chapter 2 – Understanding How The Body Heals

Only when you drink from the river of silence shall you indeed sing. And when you have reached the mountaintop, then you shall begin to climb. And when the earth shall claim your limbs, then shall you truly dance. ~ Kahlil Gibran

Kahlil Gibran gets it right again with this quotation, as I found out when I was seeking the healing power of body and mind. Silence helps considerably. That's why my special hill means so much to me, but there is also a calmness in my life now that allows me silence when my body and mind need that silence. In the mornings, when I wake earlier than others, I walk out into the garden and notice things that I used to take for granted. I see cobwebs hung in dewdrops and they look like diamond necklaces. The treasures that you find in those moments of calm recollection are valuable and help the body to heal itself.

You may not be aware of this but the human body was designed in such a way that during the hours of sleep, the body releases all that is necessary to repair damage. If you deprive yourself of sleep, you also deprive your body of the healing power of sleep. The reasons that people get ill are fairly straightforward. If the body is deprived of healing time, then the damage that occurs as a result of this deprivation is illness. Thus, although people enjoy the buzz of burning the candle at both ends, they are doing the body a disservice doing without precious sleep that helps the inner workings of the body to regenerate.

Other ways in which the body heals is to be given sufficient exercise and great nutrition. We kid ourselves that the couch potato lifestyle is the "norm" and it probably is, but the other "norm" that you need to bear in mind is the amount of people being treated with chemical medications for body ailments that occur because of this lifestyle. This book is not written to criticize anyone's lifestyle, but to show him or her the way to a better lifestyle that will make him or her healthier. Diabetes is related to sugar intake and we are all guilty of this. By regulating what you eat and by being really mindful about the eating process, you get to enjoy food more and your body gets the nutrition it needs.

The other missing element in many lives is water, and this is essential for all health aspects and needs to be incorporated into your lifestyle. Your mind will be sharper. Your body won't suffer from muscular cramps and you will feel energized if you can make these adjustments to help heal your approach to life.

The body also heals at a remarkable pace when the mind is strongly resolute and able to believe in life. When cancer patients are advised by experts, one of the most important pieces of advice is to stay positive. That is the traditionalist's way of admitting that the mind is very powerful indeed in the process of healing. If you believe that you can get beyond pain, your mind has done half of the work already and the body follows suit. Thus, those who believe that they will get better are more likely to than those who prefer to stay negative.

There's another aspect to bear in mind as well. Being spiritually aware helps you to also have the power of the mind sharpened and honed toward positivity and it is this positivity that helps considerably in the healing system. I can prove this point by citing that doctors use placebos all of the time because they know that they work. These little pills that have been tested for efficiency actually have no healing power. It is the belief in them that heals people. Thus, you can see that the healing power is within every human being on Earth if they seek it.

Self surrender to healing will take you to the top of that hill or to your chosen place of refuge and will help you to heal from illnesses because you find a new kind of contentment inside that makes you live life in a positive manner. It is this positive approach that helps you to heal. Even if your wounds are emotional, spiritual strengthening will be able to see you through all of the unhappiness toward a light that beckons you onward and helps you to heal, even when life seems to be throwing more than its fair share of curve balls.

The problem is that today people are looking for hope in all the wrong places, when true hope and healing are there for anyone to grab whenever they want it. The natural elements of nature make the air better to breathe and the colors and diversity of nature will fill your mind with the kind of awe that's hard to forget. It's not a temporary patch-up like medicines are. It's a very real and tangible healing that you can feel within you. I did and it changed my whole approach to life.

In the following chapter, I will show you how to maximize on positivity, so that you can use that special place that you choose as your point of refuge to help you gain perspective and gain a better understanding of how it all works. Once you learn these techniques, your life will become a place where you are not only happy but where you can learn to love your life and every second that happens in it. There is so much help waiting for you. You just need to know where to look. The butterfly that flew onto my hand today was the most beautiful bottle blue. Six months ago, I would not have noticed it. Since opening my eyes to life, I see the world in Technicolor and enjoy every moment of it.

Chapter 3 – Learning How To Breathe

"If your heart is a volcano, how shall you expect flowers to bloom?" ~ Kahlil Gibran

Breathing is something that you do instinctively, but do you do it in a way that helps your body? The chances are that you don't. We are in such a rush in life that we forget the importance of the way in which we breathe. If you have ever seen someone who is anxious and who is on the verge of a panic attack, the reason this happens is because their breathing is excessive and they hyperventilate. The system of breathing that I use goes hand in hand with meditation because both of these elements are useful to helping you to feel healthy and happy. As Kahlil Gibran says, you cannot expect calmness and to see the flowers bloom if you're in such turmoil that you can hear your own heartbeat.

It follows that you need to learn to breathe all over again and need to make the most of the quiet away from the world to do so. Even if you steal a moment from a busy day to give yourself a small amount of peaceful meditation, it can strengthen you and help you to cope with all kinds of circumstances. Stress is a killer. If you get into a routine of breathing correctly, you can stave off stress and also help yourself to cope when life is difficult.

Breathing and meditation exercises

Before starting to do the breathing exercises, make sure that you are sitting in a position that is comfortable. Your back needs to be straight so that your airways are clearer and breathing is improved. You also need to be in clothing that isn't constricted. Meditation helps you to get life back into perspective and that's valuable when life goes out of synch.

Breathe in through your nose and think of nothing but the breath that is entering your body. It's perhaps best to do this with your eyes closed so that you don't have external influence distracting you. Hold the breath for the count of seven, then breathe out through the nose but feel the breath coming up from the lower abdomen. Practice this several times. You need to totally concentrate on the breath. As you breathe out you can count to one, two, etc. until you reach ten. Then go back to one again. You should be able to lock out all thoughts and if they do sneak in, start back at one again.

Practice this on a regular basis because you are energizing your mind and your body and will find that you are much more functional when you are able to meditate. The healing power of the mind is amazing but you need to let it relax to do its work.

Several religions use meditation to help you to gain more insight into reaching your mind and doing so in such a way that nothing gets in the way. That gives your mind great power. When you find the benefits of meditation, try it in your chosen beauty spot and you really will feel spiritually aware. You will be able to see things more clearly and will also know your mind's capabilities and learn how much peace your mind needs for your body to feel whole and replenished.

There's a wonderful thing about sleep that you need to know. During sleep, your body goes through a period of detoxing but it can't do that unless you are able to relax enough to sleep. Being spiritually aware, you will find that you won't deprive your body of this valuable sleep because you will know inside of you that your mind needs it and your body demands it. That's not unreasonable considering the amount of stresses that you put your body through in daily life.

Meditation of this kind also makes you very aware of everything around you. You tend not to find so many faults with life and you get to be more tolerant of others, which also adds to the harmony you experience. That's worth it because it also means that you have less stress and take others into consideration as well as knowing the importance of looking after yourself properly.

When you practice the skill of breathing correctly, you also give your body all the oxygen that it needs and it's likely you will cut out a lot of bad habits because you know instantly that your body doesn't need them. I found that I stopped overdosing on caffeine because I could find enough energy within myself without needing it. Cigarettes went out the window too because I could suddenly feel that my breathing was suffering as a result of the habit and I was seeking to be happy, rather than being a slave to a drug.

Another trick that I learned with breathing was that if I introduced different aromatics into my bedroom environment, I was able to sleep the kind of sleep I hadn't slept for years and as a consequence – believe it or not – I was able to lose weight easily because of the hours I managed to sleep. Did you know that you lose weight while you sleep? You actually do if you have a balanced lifestyle. During the course of the healing process that goes on while you sleep, calories are burned at an alarmingly high rate!

Chapter 4 – The Mind Body Connection

"Truth is a deep kindness that teaches us to be content in our everyday life and share with the people the same happiness."~ Kahlil Gibran

If your mind is happy and contented, the chances are that your body has found harmony too. The mind is a powerful influence over how people feel. I remember after suffering a stroke, the right hand side of my body refused to work. My brain was still working, but I was having trouble actually getting the words out that I wanted to say. Amid all that confusion, I didn't feel ill. This was during a period when I had learned to meditate and had learned more about humility and about appreciation of nature and I knew that if I went back to my favorite place, I could help my body to heal.

Physically incapable of going back there, I still had a very vivid vision in my mind about that place and closed my eyes and absorbed it whenever I needed an extra bit of inspiration or felt that my hopes were diminishing. I know others that do this as well. There is a coherent connection between how the mind thinks and how the body responds. Look at people in hospital beds after an operation and you can perhaps see this more clearly. One person gets out of bed the day after their surgery and just gets on with life. Another patient moans at the nurses, is negative toward everyone and doesn't heal as quickly. The reason? The mind body connection demands positivity if you want it to work in a positive way. You can't be negative and complain about everything and be happy and healthy. It doesn't work. The moment that you introduce negativity, you set back your own healing.

Thus injecting positivity by thinking of that special place, I healed myself against the odds. Of course, I needed physiotherapy, but that's par for the course. However, others that had physiotherapy didn't heal. The reason for this is that there was no body mind connection. That connection that helps the healing process is most definitely associated with positive thought opening up a dialog. Negative energy blocks the dialog so that those who respond to illness in a negative way block their own potential of healing.

The next time that you are ill, close your eyes and absorb that positive space that you have chosen. Stay in it within your mind for a while and see all the cobwebs hung with dewdrops, or the rainbow that reaches across the sky in bright vibrant colors and use this to help heal you. You don't need to even think about the illness that you have in a way that insists on affirmations. It's not about affirmations. It's about using the inspiration that you find in nature to switch on the positive side of your brain that deals with healing

When you meditate or when you learn yoga, it's a mind body connection that allows you to go beyond your normal capacity. You stretch further, you breathe better, you get in touch with who you are and in this way, and you are able to help the healing process for both emotional and physical ailments.

I remember laughing at people stretching into positions that I thought looked extremely uncomfortable. What I didn't know at the time was that people who practice yoga and find flexibility are pushing their positivity to the limits so that it's always there to help them to find happiness and peace even though their lives may not be presenting them with positive opportunity. I was wrong to criticize and when I learned this, I also learned the power of healing myself in other ways than just emotionally.

My body responded to the care that I gave it but also because of the care that I gave to my mind. The mental stimulation that you give to yourself under all circumstances should always allow you to be creative, to be patient, to be empathetic and to be understanding. Once you learn to put these devices into action within the way that you think, what follows is a healing power within yourself that is very powerful.

It is something that you will have with you for always. The potential has always been there, but until you go on a voyage of discovery, you may never find that part of you that can make life happy and rewarding. Nor will you find the healing power of the mind because the mind is too busy doing other things. Imagine the mind like a pool of healing water. You have this pool outside your home. You pass by it often, but you never actually dip your foot into it and you never really appreciate what it's there for. When you do find the courage to stop thinking negatively, you allow yourself to delve into that sense of healing that we all have inside us.

You will discover that the mind is powerful and when you are able to use the power that it produces to help you in the healing process, you will not suffer as much as those who decide to leave it to medication alone. The human spirit is stronger than any medicine and helps the healing process if you allow it to.

Chapter 5 – The Past. The Future. The Present

"Yesterday is but today's memory, and tomorrow is today's dream." Kahlil Gibran

There's a lot to be said for realization that yesterday has gone. When the mind stays stuck in things that have happened, it knows no way to enjoy the moment in which you are living. I remember once being so filled with grief that I didn't notice the weather, I didn't notice the floral tributes or the pain of others. I was too filled up to brimming with my own pain. That negativity is something that people need to go through at the time of a loss, though I extended my grief. I held onto it as if it made the life of the deceased being taken justified. Of course, it didn't, and I was never going to find the road to healing until I let go of the past. I didn't know that then, but in retrospect, I could have enjoyed life a lot more than I did had I simply moved forward.

Moving forward doesn't mean that you haven't felt the sadness that was due to the occasion. It just means that you are able to find healing grace and move on in your life.

Mindfulness practice teaches us to be within the moment. That means that, as Kahlil Gibran says quite clearly, yesterday is but today's memory. It's nothing more than that, but it also needs to be said that when you live a memory, you stop all of the good things from happening in the now. I couldn't see anything good about life until nature jolted me back into reality. Driving toward the moorland, there is a point at which all the country hedges and houses disappear and you are suddenly confronted with nature in all of its glory. It was at this moment that I understood renewal. The primroses in the banks beside the road were beginning to show their flowers. The heather wasn't quite out but what it did was produce a color that is distinct across the distant hills. The sky was filled with fluffy clouds that moved across the sky and instead of thinking of negative things or about yesterday, I suddenly found myself in the moment.

That moment of natural beauty taught my mind all about renewal, about revival and about the way in which nature is so forgiving. It forgives the fact that you didn't notice what was in front of you yesterday. You were the one that suffered by not noticing. When you open your eyes to all of that splendor, you suddenly appreciate why mindfulness teaches you about living in the now.

In life, there are things that you cannot change. There are things that you know nothing about because they haven't happened yet and there are the things that are totally within your control. One of the best things that you have as a tool toward spiritual understanding is the "now." So how do you grasp it and use it to heal you? In my case, it happened all on its own the moment I discovered that the "now" was beckoning me and that it was valuable and gave me healing and happiness. For those who have not experienced this, I would say that you need to be aware of everything that is happening this moment. The sun above the trees, the bird song and the color of the leaves on the bush in the garden, the number of roses, the taste and texture of the food you eat. As soon as you put the past away – because you can't do anything to change it – and stop daydreaming about the future – because there's little you can do to control it – you start to appreciate the moment more than you ever have done in your life.

I don't just go to the beach. I feel the air in my hair. I smell the aroma of the salty seashore, I pick up the shells that offer such an array of color and I feel happy and whole. That healing process wasn't something that came naturally to me and it may not to you, but there are ways you can make it happen in a much more definite way.

- Drop thoughts about regrets and past events.

- Forgive those that you can forgive and pass responsibility to those that you cannot forgive.

- While it's okay to make short-term plans, don't live in them.

- Be aware of this moment in your life and make it count. It may be the last.

Mindfulness comes from being mindful but not many are these days. Instead, they are busy with pressing buttons on gadgets and trying to hide behind screens. I saw a couple of young girls in a park the other day and although they were together, they were not talking to each other. Neither were they aware of their surroundings. All that they were aware of was what was happening on a small screen in front of them, rather than the huge Technicolor screen of life which offered them more than a few words of badly written English that actually perplexed them, amused them or passed a moment. You could say that in their lives, they were present in the moment because their attention to their phones was so intense, although it's not the same as being mindful. Mindfulness means that you see everything around you and the beauty of it all rather than taking it for granted and seeing nothing.

You may wonder, from my saying this, whether I am saying that you should forget about technology and of course you shouldn't. It's part and parcel of everyday life, but you should try to make sure that each moment you spend is worthwhile. If that means talking to people in person instead of texting, then that's a positive move. I even use technology late at night to do my iPad crossword, but I am always very aware of the owl hooting in the back yard and the sound of the wind through the trees. You draw the line when you are forgetting to notice things that matter and substituting them with things that don't. That takes away the inner peace and it disrupts the spirituality of the moment that you are in.

As far as past is concerned, forgiving and being able to move on is essential. Each time that you remind yourself of past hurts, you may be using the excuse of protecting yourself for the future against similar things happening, but you'd be wrong. Inside you, there is this need to recall bad things that happened and to play them over in your mind. The sooner you drop them, the sooner you are able to notice the good things that surround you. How can you move forward when your thoughts are bitter and your mind is set in self-destruct mode? Similarly, those who choose to be slaves to technology are stepping away from what's real and tangible and letting themselves be pulled into a false world where they can no longer appreciate what's real and what's not. Letting the phone ring wherever you are doesn't give your mind the freedom that it needs. Imagine, you have just left work – you have had a hard day. Your bags from shopping are heavy, your bus just left without you and your stress levels are at the highest and your phone rings to add to the stress.

You need to find that place where you can escape from all of the pressures that modern life imposes sometimes, just to recharge the batteries and let the moment pass over you and caress you as a positive thing. It is always going to be that positivity that mends you and that makes you happy and contented in your life. Worries are something that you also need to drop because worries come from a very negative place indeed and do little to feed the spiritual side of who you are. It's a surface irritation that chips away at your mind and doesn't allow it to find that place of calm and peace that everyone needs.

It is hoped that within these words, you have found some neutral ground where you can discovery spiritual happiness and the power to heal your life. Your mind is working all of the time and that little bit of meditation or a visit to your favorite place on Earth can recharge the mind and make it positively energetic. The thrill of life is a wonderful thrill to embrace. Look at how a baby looks at the world and within the baby's eyes you see wonderment. The reason is that the baby hasn't yet allowed life to get in the way of actually seeing all the wonders of life. A baby is present in that moment in time. He/she sees the sunshine, the colors that surround the crib and notices all of the joys that adults seem to have long forgotten. When you find them again, hold on to them as being something dear because they are. It is all the joys that you allow into your life that feed your mind with inspiration and that allow it to heal your body.

Chapter 6 – Exercises To Take With You

From this book, you will have learned many things. You will have learned how to hone your mind to protect you from illness and from emotional stresses. It is suggested that you practice mindful meditation on a regular basis. I would suggest that quarter of an hour a day is sufficient at the beginning, but that you try to be present in each moment of your day as an intentional ploy. For example, when you wake up in the morning, embrace the weather, whatever it is. Notice the colors in the sky, the flowers that are peeking out of the border and the way in which nature is there to help you to breathe.

Enjoy life to the fullest by tasting every morsel of the food that you eat and by feeling that wonderful feeling of peace when you visit your own special place. Be gentle with yourself. That's a hard one for some people to understand but gentleness helps you to appreciate your body and your mind. Be forgiving of yourself for mistakes that you make along the way.

Meditation exercise:

In this exercise, unlike in previous meditation, you need to be aware of something wonderful within a room. This could be a vase of your favorite flowers. This isn't the best meditation to do when you are new to meditation, but after you have become accustomed to meditation practice, try it. Set the flowers down where you can see them and where you can appreciate their aroma. Seat yourself in your normal meditation position and use the flowers as something to concentrate on, disallowing any other thoughts while you go through the breathing exercises that go with meditation. Keep this up for fifteen minutes.

Observation exercise:

This helps you to see how busy the world is and how much you need to slow down to gain the best healing that you can possibly have. Sit in a street café and observe people. You don't need to talk to anyone. You just need to observe people. The reason this exercise is valid is because it makes you more empathetic toward others. Imagine yourself in the place of any one person in that café and put a positive spin on being that person. This helps you to appreciate life more and to be able to be there when friends need you to be. It's a great exercise for people seeking inner healing because it places them in someone else's shoes and lets them see the world from another viewpoint.

Physical exercising and music

Sweating it out can be particularly helpful, too. It offers a good or more positive form of 'fatigue' that can be especially good in clearing your mind and healing it from emotional burden. In this exercise, you will be required to truly pull your weight in order to achieve the healthy mind and body you deserve. Adding music to your routine can help a lot, too.

In order to fully maximize healing through physical exercise and music, you will need to get the best workout headphones. Many people take these tools for granted. However, finding yourself the best workout headphones can promote healing as well.

The best workout headphones may not always be easy to find. Although they may all seem similar, there are certain features that you may want to check before purchasing your own. For people who regularly hit the gym or run the track, it's crucial to find the right headphones that could offer them more than just the comfort they need.

The pleasure of combining workout routines and listening to music starts with finding the best pair of headphones that offers secure fit. It can get utterly frustrating to run or go biking when your earphones constantly bounce out. Adjusting them and sliding them back while cycling or using gym equipment may prove to be particularly dangerous. It is essential that you select the headphones that can keep up with your dynamic movements. There are now several types of headphone that are designed to securely stay fit throughout any given activity.

Headphones may be classified under different styles – ear hanger and ear bud. While both can be used for sports, the choice can be made on which of these two you find more stylish and more comfortable to use. The ear hanger comprises a stiff component that is placed around the ear that hangs itself, hence the name. On the other, the ear bud is the type of headphones that make use of hard plastic with customized cushion that is literally plugged into the internal part of the ear. The shapes and sizes may differ, but these best workout headphones are all designed ergonomically.

Some contain silicone pieces to keep them fit and in place even amid fast movements.

The inclusion of in-lined controller and microphone

It is no longer surprising to see athletes using their smart phones during intense workouts. Their phones get to be their music players, a source of entertainment, and a pedometer. With these multiple functions, an in-line microphone and an in-line controller can be especially useful. These are also among the basic features that the best workout headphones have. The controllers may allow you to execute quick adjustment to the volumes, pause, skip, replay certain podcasts or music files.

Moreover, the inclusion of microphone can be practical should you wish to take or make a quick call while in the middle of the workout routine. For people on the go, these two features are a must. Thus, the versatility of workout headphone is becoming more and clearer now. For others, they also prefer to use the best workout headphones that have Bluetooth capabilities.

Choosing the best workout headphones may also depend on the type of activities you do. If you are keen on running, mountain biking, skiing, or any sport that need speed, you may want to choose the headphones that also have a 'tangle-resistance' feature. This can help you drop the need to regularly untangle the cords while in the middle of a routine. Another option is to get yourself the headphones model with shorter or adjustable cords. Ultimately, the best workout headphone should give you the utmost comfort you may need. With comfort and the right amount of music and exercise, you can ensure that healing is in the works.

Chapter 7 - Identifying The Barriers That Delay Healing

Pain may stem from various causes. It attacks the different facets of one's life. It can strike anyone-- kids, adult, the elderly, and even the newborn. The result is -- management of the pain becomes more specialized. But there are methods that will enable you to get understand the root cause of the pain so you can properly and methodically weed it out from your system.

Healing takes time. Healing is a process. But to ensure that healing takes place smoothly, it is essential to determine the barriers that cordon you off from total transformation. What keeps you stuck and what halts the healing process your mind and body need? Moreover, understanding these barriers would help your mind and body accept the positive changes.

Top Three Barriers That Could Hinder Complete Healing of the Mind and Body:

1. Painful childhood experiences

Healing recurring pain that would not seem to go away may be caused by childhood experiences. The absence of accountability when the painful experience happened serves as a permanent market that scars a person for a long time. The assessment of the pain is highly recommended. Focus should also be placed on how to identify these experiences. A look back in the past would trigger more pain. This is where professional help is needed. For younger individuals inflicted with childhood pains, the following points should be kept in mind:

• Both the developmental stage and age be used as factors in assessing pain in younger individuals

• The attenuation of anxiety and pain may be performed through a combine mind-body and medical procedures

• Pain experienced by children is usually under treated or misinterpreted

• Different Mind-body therapies are likewise recommended for treating recurring pain syndromes that include headaches and abdominal pains

2. Recurring negative thoughts

The build-up of negative thoughts cloud your judgment, thinking, as well as weaken your ability to get out of it. Rumination or the rehashing of negative thoughts can lead to condition even worse than addiction. It can likewise be extremely counterproductive for some as it literally take up so much energy and time. The worst case scenarios are that people may eventually experience long-term or chronic depression.

Healing becomes more difficult if you continue to dwell on these negative thoughts. As renowned psychologists Guy Winch, Ph.D mentioned in his book, "Emotional First Aid, " the presence of negative thoughts is tantamount to a 'needle in one groove'. This means that asthe negative thoughts build up, the groove becomes deeper which could stuck the needle and it tougher to get out of the deepe groove.

The negative thoughts are likewise a huge roadblock to emotional healing. They can turn an angry person to an even angrier individual. Every minor problem you encounter becomes magnified. And as time goes by, the negative thoughts continue to zap your energy, you become weaker and weaker to the point that healing becomes nearly impossible.

In order to avoid the worst case scenarios, you can try the following techniques that can help you fight back those negative thoughts and steer clear from rumination:

• Keep a healthy and positive social circle. As a popular adage states, "It only takes one rotten tomato to spoil the bunch." This is true as human behavior can be highly infectious, too. In order to cordon yourself off the sources of negative thoughts, be selective of the people you spend time with. In one study published in 2013 by researchers from the University of Notre Dame, younger individuals pick up negative behaviors from roommates. Keep ample distance from these people who you believe are perpetually negative.

• Keep healthy distractions like going shopping or thinking of your dream holidays. Replacing thoughts can be a good way to get rid of the negative ones. If you find yourself starting to feel submerged in a pile of negative thoughts, you can quickly change it by visualizing yourself inside your favorite shop or a dream vacation destination. Think of the activities you can do while in your pretend holiday destination. You may also opt to do something that requires extensive concentration. For example, remembering the names of your former teachers, the order of songs on your play list, or the books on yourself, could all help you replace the negative ideas to more positive ones.

• Get warmer. Negative thoughts have various sources and identifying all of them may be quite tedious to do. However, researchers have found that going for anything physically warm can actually provide your comfort during times of loneliness and pain. Using a hot pack and placing on a physical pain, going for a warm shower, or having a cup of warm tea can all provide a quick fix. So if negative thoughts start to dawn on you, maybe it is the best time to ring a friend and have warm cup of coffee over warm conversations.

• Throwing and crashing can offer emotional relief, too. Though this may sound over-the-top, psychologists have always recommended the trick of writing down your stressors or anything that triggers emotional pain and negative thoughts on the paper. Next thing to do is to tear the paper apart, crumple the pieces, and throwing them away on trash bin. A similar study was conducted by the Ohio State University back in 2012, and results were positively uncanny. The respondents who did the exercise of writing down their negative thoughts and stressors, and got those paper binned, have gained a better self-image and more positive demeanor just as few minutes after.

• Re framing your current situation and see the 'silver lining' in it. It is too easy for people to feel frustrated and dwell on negative thought when in a bad situation. For example, if you missed your plane because you got caught in a traffic jam, you will certainly feel bad about it. But instead of crying over spilled milk, think of the other things you can do instead. You have an extra day to discover the city. You have time to call up friends and family while waiting for your next flight. AS they say, it is all about perspective.

To conquer the negative thoughts in your mind may appear as though you are trying to beat a virtual Goliath. In fact, you can be just as smart and as determined as 'David'. All it takes it your willpower and your genuine desire to heal your mind and body.

3. **Uncleared Traumas**

Healing should also cover the healthy management of uncleared traumas a person may have. Lasting traumas have a fundamental impact on the life as well as on the psychological outlook of the person. Catastrophes such as warm terrorism, natural disasters, and even painful experiences caused by loved ones are among the toughest barriers to beat when aiming at complete healing. These sad and anger-bearing reminders of the past leave some lasting scars that put the healing process to halt. A person who is badly inflicted with uncleared traumas as described to be 'frozen in time'.

Healing these traumas require a painful yet effective confrontation. Many people believe, including a number of experts that banishing these memories from consciousness is one of the immediate responses to atrocities. A sturdy and efficient psychological restoration is an important component of healing. Survivors must be provided with a space where they would feel genuinely heard. Being able to utter aloud these atrocities from the past would help healing to proceed, as survivors would be able to acknowledge the events as catalysts for their personal rebirth. Moreover, the eradication and healing of these traumas would likewise contribute to the rebuilding of a person's social life.

The healing process of those with uncleared traumas require three very important steps, namely:

- **Formulating a feeling of 'safety'.** Putting victims in a place where they are given the utmost feeling safety would enable them to slowly yet effectively reveal the details of what had happened to them. Retelling the ordeal is never easy, but is found to be one of the most therapeutic ways of getting rid of the pain.

- **Acknowledgment of the event.** This is the second step of the process and can be achieved when the story of the traumatic event is successfully retold in the presence of someone who the victim trusts.

- **The third part is the re-connection.** This can be achieved once the victims gets to forgive herself as well as accept the apology of the other party.

Chapter 8 - Healing Depression

Depression is one of the conditions that need a lot of attention. This does not occur overnight and the healing process requires time as well. The truth about depression is that despite a number of studies and publicity about it, it remains as one of the enigmatic psychological conditions to date. People who suffer from this disease judge themselves and get drowned with shame everyday.

Contrary to what people believe, depression is not just about feeling sad or very sad. Depression also entails being helpless and hopeless, and having the odd feeling that everything else will fail. Even in the simplest situations, a depressed person may feel overly pessimistic. Healing this kind of mental condition has been the subject of countless studies.

A person who is diagnosed with depression does not only have a single disorder. A person experiences collective signs and symptoms before a real diagnosis can be made. Here are some of the symptoms that a potential sufferer may demonstrate for at least two weeks:

•Significant weight loss even when making effort

- Significant loss of interest in anything (e.g. work, studies, friends, hobbies, etc.)

- Feeling a sense of emptiness and numbness

- Slow production of thoughts

- Being inactive and the tendency to space out all the time

- Getting passive aggressive

- Becoming indecisive

- Frequent exhaustion even from lack of activity

- Overly quiet

- Contemplating on suicide or running away

- Thinking of death

- Lack of sleep or too much sleep

Taking the First Steps of Healing

Re-balancing your self so as to heal completely is possible, but will require time, efforts, and a lot of support. If people started to show genuine concern over your behavior and if someone had asked you if you feel depressed, then take these two as very important signs that you, in fact, need help. Check with a doctor to see if there are medical conditions that may have brought about your depression such as vitamin deficiencies, chronic pains, thyroid dysfunction or others. Understand and expect that the truth may hurt at first, but this is ultimately the first step of healing.

1. Restoring the balance through traditional yoga

When people are coping with any form of emotional pain, the use of intellectual approach proves to be insufficient. A depressed person may continue to be trapped in his own emotional prison and staying there would only intensify the negative emotions and continue to ruin the balance.

Through yoga, you can command both your body and mind to take part in the process of healing. Yoga can be instrumental to a transformation that through the unity of body, mind, and spirit. Through yoga, a person suffering from both mental and physical pain may experience a restful awareness and emotional balance.

Yoga can expedite healing as it helps in the release of the so-called emotional blockages. Pains are also caused by the sudden shifts in the human body's chemistry. This is a point when you start to feel physical pains as caused by the disturbance on the hormonal balance. The physiological shifts trigger emotional outbursts that ultimately destroy the mind-body systems of the body.

Healing through yoga can be achieved by listening well and paying attention to the changes and sensations you feel in your body. This would aid you in locating the areas where tension has to be released. Of course, the practice, however, must be facilitated and lead by a trained and experience yoga teacher.

2. Examining your response mechanism

Being helpless and enduring the adverse and lasting effects of depression all begin with reaction. The habit of fundamentally offering a self-defeating kind of response is the first a person takes when unable to fight the plight of depression. Most of the time, people find this aspect irrelevant, but experts reiterate that the way we react to difficult situations often triggers the build up of negative thoughts.

Here are certain alternatives you can try when you feel like to reacting negatively:

- •Instead of saying, "I am not good enough", you may replace this with, and "I am just as lovable, just as free, and just as good as others." You can continue by saying out loud, "I should stop comparing myself to other people. I am different. But I am good."

- •Instead of saying, " I can never get out of this," you can tell yourself, " I should open my eyes and see all the new possibilities each day has to offer." Continue on by reminding yourself all of the achievements you have had over the years.

- •Instead of saying, " Nothing ever will work out," you can tell yourself, " There's always good in everything. I may not see it now, but I believe things will fall into place." Failure is an opportunity to do something again, something better.

Recognizing these prompt depressing responses will help you learn new expressions that will also accelerate the healing process. These affirmations will eventually train your mind to counter any negative response automatically and help you build a more positive pattern of thinking, something more nurturing and healthy.

Chapter 9 - Healing Body Pains

Body pain is considered one of the most common kind of pains experienced by people as young as 20 years old and as old as 70. As per the American Pain Foundation, this condition is likewise one of the main reasons people see doctors on a regular basis. Although body pain may not necessarily severe all the time, it is also considered as one of the most difficult conditions to treat.

For many people, going under the knife or dabbling in any evasive procedure may be an option. However, experts such as Dr. Anders Cohen of Brooklyn Hospital Center, New York strongly believe that the majority of these people does not really need or will not benefit from surgeries.

The lower back is seen as a complex spot that is prone to different kinds of pains. On the contrary, it likewise offers a range of opportunities for different forms of therapies. The alternative medicinal approach is often given to patients with healthy discs or backbones. This alternative approach is commonly offered to people whose chronic condition may stem from weak muscles or tissues connected to the bone.

Here are the top alternatives in medicinal approach in addressing back problems:

1. Chiropractic therapy

It is a false impression that chiropractors are only capable of treating problems by 'cracking the back' of the patients. In fact, these health practitioners are also trained to treat soft tissue problems in the back. Moreover, through chiropractic therapy, the pain that is felt radiating from the lower back down to the buttocks, hips and upper legs can also be treated.

This therapy may also involve the use of sonogram and combining it with ample heat to cure muscle spasms and to identify the trigger points that could lead to chronic irritation. The 'cracking of the back' method is also helpful in treating back problems as it aids in re-balancing the spine. This is done when nitrogen bubbles from the spine are released right in the joints.

2. Pilates

You may have already read how yoga helps a lot in managing your back problems. To top it off, you may also opt to try Pilates. This technique from Germany is also now advised to those suffering from chronic lower back problems as it can zap the lingering pain.

Pilates is particularly helpful for back problems as it involves techniques that can help both strengthen the spine and the tissues. These techniques include muscle strengthening, coordinating strength, body coordination, breathing and body symmetry. Pilates also helps the patient retain good body alignment that can make you become more resistant to fatigue, injury, and pain in general. The principle behind Pilates is to strengthen the core of the body as well as the hips. By achieving a strong and toned core, the back gets the relief it needs when lifting weights. Thus, it assures the back against the usual wear-and-tear injury it could experience.

It is important to note, however, that this particular alternative approach cannot be performed by people with herniated disks. There are flexibility exercises that are found counterproductive to people that experience spine changes. This practice may increase the stress fracture in the spine and may hamper its rehabilitation.

3. Temperature

There is a good reason why using hot/cold compress is often used as a first-aid treatment. The variable temperature helps in reducing pain and potential inflammation. The same principle can also be applied to manage lower back problems.

• The Cold Therapy

This method has two main benefits. One is that it immediately reduces back inflammation. Secondly, it has an anesthetic effect. Such an effect can slow down the impulses of the nerves that also reduces the likelihood of experiencing pain and spasm. Cold therapy can be done by making homemade ice/gel packs. Keeping an ice pack in the fridge can offer instant relief should lower back pain strikes.

• The Heat Therapy

This method has also two different benefits. Firstly, heat can stimulate the flow of the blood that allows nutrients to be delivered and absorbed in the affected area. Secondly, it also slows down the triggering of the 'pain messages' and stops them from being sent to the core of the nervous system -- the brain. Using heat can be done in various manners. The use of heating pad and bottle with hot water among the simplest ways. You may also benefit from heat by soaking in a tub with warm water or by taking a warm shower.

4. Brainwork

Pain is not just a mere sensation-- this is one of its properties that many pain specialists have been making sense of. The pain one person feels depends on how the brain interprets and perceives the sensation. Thus, the brain process pains signals that can make people feel the physical aspect of pain.

Now, there are certain therapies that can help you ignore the pain signals. You can actually manipulate how your brain processes these signals and develop the right skills on how you can reduce the pain signals. Going through these therapies can help you have more influence over the potential pain you could feel.

5. Aerobic Exercises

Aerobics is an excellent option for those chronic back problems, but not for those degenerated discs. One of the best benefits of doing aerobics is that such exercise can strengthen the tissues and muscles in the back area when done on a regular basis. Health care practitioners also suggest brisk walking for people who constantly experience lower back pain. This is because walking offers a more natural position for the spine than sitting itself. When a person sits, particularly in a low chair, the spine experiences a curvature that could aggravate the pain and the strain.

6. Restorative Sleep

Time and time again, people are advised to have enough sleep to improve overall health condition. It has been found that almost 60% of the people experiencing chronic back problems also suffer from a form of sleep disorder. This could also mean that having an inadequate amount of sleep could escalate pain in the back. Therefore, treating both the back pain and the sleep disorder could be beneficial.

Sleep problems that come with back problems can also be treated using the following methods:

- Relaxation method

- Medication

- Cutting back on sugar and caffeine

- Psychological techniques

7. Psychological Therapies

When chronic conditions become unbearable for patients, the condition itself becomes more 'psychological' than physical. This could very well happen if the causes of the back pain become too difficult to detect.

In these cases, there are psychological therapies that are recommended for patients to undergo. The main purpose is to reset the mind of a patient as well as to help him refocus more on finding solutions that will ease the pain. Examples of these treatments are hypnosis, cognitive behavioral therapy, and hypnosis.

Now that you have learned the alternative approach to dealing with your back problems effectively, it would be better to also gain knowledge on how you can truly boost the treatment with different natural supplements.

Chapter 10 - Cultivating Self-Love And Self-Respect

Every waking moment of every day, we generally want to be at our best – physically, mentally, spiritually, and emotionally. BUT in reality, how many of us can honestly say that we are truly happy from within when we look at ourselves in the mirror every morning? Maybe some people are, but the question is – ARE YOU ONE OF THEM? If yes, then you should take the first step to learning how to cultivate self-love and self-respect as part of the healing process.

Body image is fundamentally described as how you see yourself from the outside. The unrealistic perception of how you see your entire body in front of the mirror is referred to the distorted body image. Most of the time, the negative body image is fuelled by size, physical flaws, and low self-esteem. Getting inundated by criticisms from peers, friends, and even family members also add up to your perception of your entire body image.

With all these in mind, one of the major culprits of poor body image is the presence of psychological disorders Yes, it is not just FOOD that should be regarded as the primary reason, but how perceive ourselves and how we choose to portray ourselves in the eyes of others matter, too.

Have you noticed yourself being overly dependent on food and vices in relieving stress, handling emotions, and escaping from other issues? Do you often torture yourself with the impression of being 'ugly', 'fat', and 'unwanted'? Do you dread the idea of seeing yourself, your silhouette, or merely your face on the mirror, on the wall, or on photos? Do you constantly blame others, your pain, and your personal struggles for your overall appearance? If you happen to answer all these questions with a resounding YES, then you know that you do have a real problem to address, treat, and manage.

Being unable to own up to these issues can result in a cycle of destructive behaviors and other linked disorders. Depriving yourself of the real treatment can be detrimental to your overall health. Failing to understand the onset of your psychological problems may eventually obliterate your capacity to have a positive outlook.

Body and Mind problems can be healed. This is the first thing that you should bear in mind. Although they are remediable, they also require long-term management and willpower so you can be free from them as you go on with your life.

Once you have learned to love yourself a little bit more, you are actually freeing yourself from all the worries and the handicaps brought about by physical and mental pains. Respecting yourself would also help you to offer yourself more liberating options on how to live a life that is healthier from within.

In order to cultivate self-respect ad self-love, you need to remember that pain and its countless forms are not a reason to completely cordon yourself off from the public. Running away from it is tantamount to heading straight back to it. That's how vicious it is. On the contrary, it should be perceived as an opportunity for you to increase your personal awareness to how you can take care of yourself better by guarding both your thoughts and your actions.

You may find yourself in an endless battle of healing any kind of pain. However, the mere presence of it should be considered as indication that many of our habits, the way we perceive things, and the mode we choose to cope with any circumstance may have drastic impact on our health – physically and mentally.

If you strongly believe that you are yet to complete the process of healing, then you must commend yourself for having been able to detect abnormalities in your own behavior. Running away from the reality of any disorder is sometimes an option that some sufferers take. This will not help at all! To sum up how to win the battle against any given disorder you need to prepare your body and mind to embrace three things: GET HELP, BE INVOLVED, and STAY EDUCATED. Healing requires your action, too!

There is absolutely no shame in getting the professional help that you need. From self-help tips to something more socially acceptable, and to a range of science-based treatments – you can certainly find one that suits you the best. Remember that, in healing the mind and the body, the adage 'One Size Fits All' does not apply! The moment you start starving yourself from the real help that support groups and a professional therapist can give is tantamount to subjecting yourself to the worst mental torture ever. So why choose to suffer?

Being involved is expected in two areas – being committed in your treatment, and being part of the recovery of other people. Your true commitment, as well as active participation, can yield drastic changes in your conditions. Your precious time can likewise be instrumental in helping those who are trying to heal from physical and emotional pains who are in dire need of support. Being involved in the healing of others could very well mean

Staying educated is likewise a powerful tool that will ensure better lifestyle choices, improved thinking patterns, and strong will in making decisions linked with the recovery and complete healing. The information will not automatically be fed to you, but you will have to stay extra vigilant in keeping yourself updated.

Life will continue to become a blessing no matter how tough your struggle is as long as you choose it to live it that way. Everything you do – from the time the pain begins to the point where you are ready to finally completely heal – all of these highly depend on YOU. Know that you deserve a better life, better health, better habits, better thoughts, and better communities. To get these you know that you need to ACT ON IT!

Self-control plays a vital role in the process and must be taken into account in any activity. Live life with moderation and openness to healing – these are the key! Do not allow yourself to continuously live with a huge amount of toxicity and complexity because of lack of self-love and self-respect . The keywords you need to remember are SELF-AWARENESS and POSITIVITY. These will allow you to embark on a whole new life.

Chapter 11 - Mind And Body Healing Against Eating Disorders

No matter how pleasurable and satisfying – anything excessive or too minimal is bad for you. Whether it pertains to work, hobbies, interests, cigarettes or food, taking and doing things in moderation is a must.

Healing Begins with Understand of the Conditions

Eating disorders are different in nature. These are conditions that require complete healing of both the mind and the body. Someone who suffers from any eating disorder consumes an abnormal amount of food and experiences an uncontrollable desire to eat more and more or less and less. Eating excessively results in guilt that then prompts the sufferer to eat again. Thus, a vicious cycle of ensues.

Among the first known eating disorder was the Night Eating Disorder (NES) based on a study conducted by a psychiatrist named Albert Stunkard back in 1959. However, NES was eventually reclassified as Binge eating as patients had also displayed the same behavior even in a non-nocturnal environment.

Among the similarity in behavior demonstrated by sufferers of eating disorders are the presence of guilt, anxiety, disgust, and depression. This blanket of negative emotions often pushes the sufferers to eat more, therefore creating a vicious cycle of eating for relief.

Mere overeating vs. Eating Disorders

Do you hate the Christmas season because you tend to eat more and gain extra pounds after? Do you always find it enticing you have another slice of cake for dessert when you know for a fact that you are already full? Do you tend to eat again even just after having your lunch or dinner? Do you also like the idea trying out new dishes or exploring new restaurants regularly? Well, most of us do, but that does qualify us on binge eating spree.

Overeating is a natural tendency for people to have an extra cup of rice, an extra slice of cake, or another bite of chocolate even when they already feel satiated or full. This often happens during periods of enjoyment and celebrations such as Christmas dinners, going on a late night out with friends, birthday lunches, etc. On the contrary, Binge Eating is a real disorder that can be diagnosed, measured, and treated. The latter often occurs in an impulsive manner, particularly when the sufferer aims to conceal an emotional downturn or when a triggering factor arises. Any eating disorder is often accompanied by guilt, blues, hatred, depression, and other emotional distress. People who have poor body image of themselves also undergo physical distress that could trigger the eating disorder. In short, binge eating is a condition that is just as bad as other eating disorders more commonly known such as Anorexia Nervosa and Bulimia Nervosa. It can be truly fatal if left untreated or undetected.

The term Binge Eating Disorder is further defined by the American Psychiatric Association (APA) as the consumption of a significantly larger amount of food within a short period of time. The urge to eat more could also happen on a recurring basis. The uncontrollable behavior sets it apart from just merely overeating.

The three main criteria for eating disorders according to The Diagnostic and Statistical Manual of Mental Disorders, 5th Edition (DSM-5) of the American Psychiatric Association (APA) are the following:

- Loss of control on the amount of food taken

- Evident distress experienced pre and post binge episodes

- Abnormal eating that happens at least once a week for a period of one-quarter of a year

It has been found that binge eating is far more common than any other eating disorders such as Bulimia Nervosa and Anorexia Nervosa. APA also reveals that roughly 5 million women struggle with this disorder. Moreover, about 3 million of men in the US have also been diagnosed with this illness. The Institute also believes that there more than 10 million of cases. However, as the condition often goes undetected, several sufferers fail to acquire suitable treatments. The next chapters will walk you through on the factors and the symptoms of eating disorders.

Heal Yourself from the Myths on Eating Disorders

Eating disorders can be very confusing to many. The idea of eating a lot is interpreted by many people differently – emotional eating, gluttony or merely overeating.

The following are the typical myths thrown at sufferer of these eating disorders. Before you become a victim, start educating yourself on what is true about this eating disorder. It is also by education that you can avoid becoming a sufferer yourself.

Myth #01: Eating Disorders are not really 'disorders'

Fact #01: Well, it is and a number of people can attest to this. Once in a while we let loose of ourselves during Christmas or Thanksgiving. We eat more than what our body needs. That's fine, as it only happens about once or twice a year. On the other hand, a Binge Eating Disorder sufferer tends to do this at least twice a week in a period of 3 months – sometimes even longer. This is a disorder and is highly linked with the general psychological health of a person. Sad, but true.

Myth #02: Anorexia is not as serious as Bulimia Nervosa.

Fact #02: Not at all. They are both disorders that require treatment. Although in both cases, the sufferers tend to binge on a large amount of food. The main difference though is that an anorexic does not purge while a bulimic person does. Purging can be done by forcing oneself to vomit. Laxatives, water pill, and too much exercising are also the other means by which a bulimic person gets rid of the extra calories taken.

Myth #03: Eating disorders are only for women especially when they are stressed, dumped, or when they feel bad about something.

Fact #03: Although most eating disorders are more common to women, men are not completely immune to eating disorders in general. Eating disorders should not also be mistaken with emotional eating. With eating disorders, the depression, anxiety, and stress escalate even after eating food. However, an emotional eater tends to find 'comfort' with food.

Myth #04: Binge eating sufferers are all obese.

Fact#04: Although it is one of the potential consequences, many of the binge eating sufferers are not overweight at all. Those who undergo this problem come in different sizes, genders, and medical conditions. Treatment of binge eating is also put in place in order to suppress the possible occurrence of other health impacts such obesity, diabetes, sleep apnea, gastrointestinal problems, and more.

Myth #05: Eating disorders are a rare condition.

Fact #05: This may be surprising, but there is more binge eating disorder cases than other eating disorders such as anorexia and bulimia. There are about 5-10 million of cases of BED cases in the US and the number increases every year. Many BED cases, for example, go also go undetected.

Myth #06: Teenagers are more prone to Eating Disorders.

Fact #06: Although eating disorders are more common to women of 25 years old and above, there are roughly 1.6% of teens experiencing this. As for men, it most occurs during their mid-life. There are now support groups and eating disorder clinics for young teens who may be suffering from any form of eating disorder.

Myth #07: Bulimia is easy to resolve; Anorexia is far more dangerous

Fact #07: There is no such thing as 'easy' for any eating disorder. Bulimia, anorexia, and other eating disorder all pose dangers to health if not addressed or treated properly. Secondary conditions like depression, bipolar disease, PTSD, and even dementia may develop from these. As mentioned earlier, hypertension and Type 2 Diabetes are also among the health consequences.

Myth #08: No one can heal from eating disorders

Fact #08: Not anymore. One of the most recent medical breakthroughs is the use of a particular medicine that can now be given to sufferers of eating disorders. If you wish to know more about it, you may check it in one of the next chapters. This is certainly good news to all those who have languished with this eating disorder.

Myths are the typical barriers to recovery. Eradicating them will allow sufferers to fully understand their situations and to let the healing process start. The earlier these myths are explained to the sufferers, the easier it will be for them to focus on the healing process.

Get to Know the Eating Disorder's Root Causes

Yes, FOOD! This is the main tool that Eating Disorder sufferers use to demonstrate their weaknesses. However, it should be highlighted that although the disorder is mainly manifested through food, it is not exactly the culprit. By nature, an eating disorder is a psychiatric issue that can be treated by addressing the mental and emotional struggles of a person.

Early detection of eating disorders is also essential for the early treatment, and to avoid the development of further medical conditions such as obesity, diabetes, hypertension, etc. Understanding the causes of this condition is just as important as knowing the treatments available to date.

The development of eating disorders is highly dependent on the following factors:

Factor #01: **BIOLOGICAL**

Eating Disorders may be caused by certain abnormalities in the biological makeup of a person. Studies have found that compulsive eating may also be caused by genetic mutations and certain hormonal irregularities. These are also to be blamed for the development of another eating disorder – food addiction.

Factor #02: **SOCIAL**

Eating Disorders can also stem from sexual abuse and other traumatic experiences. Emotional eating can highly develop from social stressors such as the pressure to look like models and emulate celebrities. Being involved in a critical situation where a person feels hopeless may likewise increase a person's chances of falling into the trap of eating disorders such as Anorexia, Bulimia, and Binge Eating. Being born from a family of dysfunctional dynamic is also one of the most common causes

Factor #03: **PSYCHOLOGICAL**

Eating Disorders can also be the by-product of anxiety and depression. A strong correlation between these two has been established by a series of studies and research. Having poor coping mechanisms and diminishing self-esteem are also among the top catalysts of the condition.

Taking the Signs and Symptoms Seriously

Binge Eating Disorder, just like other eating-related problems, is complex by nature. Its development may be linked to several factors, but the real cause often goes undetected and even unexplained.

Complex as it may truly seem, it also offers a range of signs and behavioral symptoms that you should be keen on addressing. If you suspect that a loved one's overeating is fueled by the following factors, then start seeking for an eating disorder specialist for tests and treatments:

●Noticing someone to eat continually even when he or she is already full

●Hoarding food to be consumed secretly when no one seems to be watching

●Feeling of numbness when consuming a large amount of food

●Unceasing urge to eat more and more

●Unable to reach the feeling of 'satiation' or being full

• Eating normal amount of food when in the presence of other people, but tends to eat too much when alone

• Reaching out for food immediately when feeling stressed, sad, or anxious

• Unable to control the type of food to be eaten, will eat whatever is in the fridge, on the table, etc

Another obvious characteristic of a binge eater is having that feeling of guilt right after consuming an enormous amount of food. This guilt could then trigger back his or her appetite which may likewise lead to another episode of overeating. Thus, a cycle occurs.

What could possibly happen if Binge Eating Disorder is not addressed immediately?

The clear consequence of eating disorders is gaining unwanted or unnecessary weight which could also branch into worse condition – obesity. Thus, this condition may likely result in a set medical problems including:

• Type 2 Diabetes

• Hypertension

• Cardiovascular problems

• Gastrointestinal issues

• Insomnia

• Sleep apnea

• Gallbladder problems

• Severe depression

- Muscular pain

- Joint pain

- Back problems

Healing through the Acceptance of Medical Breakthroughs

A new drug was approved by the United States Food and Drug Administration (FDA) in January 2015 that has the generic name of <u>lisdexamfetamine dimesylate.</u> This specific drug has the brand name of *Vyvanse*. The main purpose of the drug is to cure adults suffering from Binge Eating Disorder. This is now considered a medical breakthrough, as the drug happens to be the first of its kind that is intended to treat the said eating disorder.

Before the approval of the United States Food and Drug Administration (FDA), the researchers who were involved in the study had presented their findings using a poster at the annual meeting of the American Psychiatric Association (APA).

The study involved 270 random participants in the two-phase double-blind method. There were also additional 266 participants in the efficacy analysis stage. The participants also underwent a screening phase for 2 weeks to ensure that they would demonstrate binge eating behavior for at least 3 days each week. The participants were in their late 30s and had Body Mass Index of 25-35.

The participants who received LDX treatment were reported to have demonstrated better control over their eating habits as well as improved cognitive restraint.

However, before you jump up and down out of happiness, it is important to also emphasize that the use of the abovementioned medicine requires utmost care and guidance by your therapists or doctors. As in any other drugs, it also has counter indication and may pose allergic reactions. Consulting your doctor about it is highly advised.

It is also important to reiterate that there are a number of professional researchers/organizations that aim to provide more cures to Binge Eating Disease as well as to other eating disorders. It can be expected that sooner, there could be a new range of treatment and approach to finally say adieu to eating disorders. Let's keep our hopes us. Yes, optimism works.

A Few Clicks Away from Getting the Professional Help You Need

Hooray! So you have finally convinced yourself to get the professional help you need. Well, congratulations! This is the first step and you have taken it with all courage and might. The heaing process has truly unfolded. If you are not quite sure where to start, you may want to check the following tools on the Internet to start your journey to recovery right away.

Yes, this time, you are allowed to browse the Web for more help. In fact, you can immediately get yourself familiarized with the organizations below. So happy browsing and we certainly hope that you will find the right place for you!

Anonymous. If you want to get engage in the self-help group, you may check Overeaters Anonymous that may be present in your community. The group makes use of 12 keys in recovering from Binge Eating Disorder. You can make new friends and also learn from what they have experienced. It is also an ideal place to start as you will be given the opportunity to learn also from their system at your own pace.

The Eating Disorder Referral and Information Center. If you are looking for a comprehensive database of treatment providers for eating disorders such as Binge Eating, then go straight ahead to The Eating Disorder Referral and Information Center. The database of the group is easy to navigate and you can also narrow down your searches.

Eating Disorders Anonymous. Just like the first group mentioned, there is also another self-help group called Eating Disorders Anonymous. The group offers support and a number of group meetings. You can quickly check if they have a group available in your area by checking their website.

The Something Fishy Website on Eating Disorders For the complete directory of eating disorder clinics, dietitians, therapists, specialists, and support facility/groups, you can search The Something Fishy Website on Eating Disorders.

The Academy for Eating Disorders. This is an association founded by professionals that are committed to conducting thorough research on eating disorders, prevention, treatment, and education as a whole. You can easily find news and updates on the treatments and the possibilities of new curative measures in the future.

Eating Disorders Coalition. This Washington-based organization aims to promote awareness as well educate policymakers on the life-threatening impacts of eating disorders. Their goal is also to make eating disorder among the priorities for public health management.

NORMAL in Schools, Inc. This is a national nonprofit organization that aims to educate people about eating disorders, managing self-esteem, and positive body image through the use of arts and a set of mindfulness programs. You may want to inquire on how to avail any of their programs. Mindfulness programs are also among the top approach in dealing with behavioral issues. Get in touch with the group and get further motivated by their responses.

You can jumpstart your search towards your recovery via any of the websites above. Remember that when dealing with eating disorder, self-medicating is NEVER the answer. Make full use of the resources you can find.

Chapter 12 - Self- Healing Through Dancing

If you happen to know someone who has been dealing with lingering pain and with an incredible passion for dancing, then the problem is ALMOST solved.

One of the least known therapies for both physical and psychological diseases is the use of dancing skills. Uncanny as it may sound, but dancing is found to be one of the most effective therapies that can be utilized as a healing process. This now called – Dance Movement Therapy.

Dance Movement Therapy

This form of therapy is used by many experienced psychologists and is carried out by providing the patients with an opportunity to perform guided movement. It is also considered as one of the most creative outlets for emotional expressions that many people in pain long to have. This therapy is likewise known to be an efficient form of psychotherapy for other conditions such as autism, mental retardation, learning disabilities, and even dementia. Many eating disorder clinics and rehabilitation centers also offer dance therapy to potential patients.

Four Stages of the Dance Movement Therapy

Stage #01: Preparation where the patients are required to do warm-up exercises and stretching

Stage #02: Incubation where the patients learn to relax and become more mindful

Stage#03: Illumination or the stage where symbolism is learned as well as the effects of each movement

Stage #04: Evaluation or the stage where the patient processes and conclude the session

Finding solutions to your condition need not to be boring and very conventional. Sometimes, we can use 'happier' approaches to lighten up the road to recovery. As you inch your way back to your healthier self, do not forget to take your dancing shoes with you.

Chapter 13: Holding On While Healing

The journey to full recovery is truly a painstaking one. Pain may strike more than once in the entire lifetime, so management is paramount. Recovery does not happen overnight, and people who undergo long-term therapies may find the treatments equally stressful. This is where family and friends are needed most.

Months and probably even years of treatment require a load of commitment to maintaining full recovery. The tricky part of having to experience any form of pain is that relapse is constantly lurking. Long-term management is truly a hard work that can also be sustained through determination, mindfulness, awareness, and again, commitment.

It is also just as important now to know keeps 'on the wagon' of a healthy lifestyle. Instead of fearing the idea that the pain will trigger once again, you may want to divert your thoughts on how you can continually embrace healthier eating habits. Here are some helpful tips that can win your way back to your healthier self again:

- **Be aware of your own support system.** Being surrounded with people who genuinely care for you and are there to accompany you on your way towards recovery. If you have reached a point where you feel like relapsing, go to a specific person directly and tell him or her your concern. Being able to trust someone with your weaknesses is helpful as she or he can immediately offer any kind of support to help you get over the temptations. Families and friends are usually among the first people to give you the right kind of support. However, you may also trust someone from the local community or a self-help group.

- **Understand what triggers the pain.** Assess yourself and your own behavior. Identify what pushes you re-engaged in poor eating habits. Most of the time, it is a particular emotion or circumstance, so be mindful of these triggering factors. If you think being sad makes you constantly hungry, then take some actions to feel happy instead. A strong willpower is essential in handling these factors well. Your coping mechanism will also be strengthened if you are able to discover the culprits behind your behavior. Journalizing, in this case, is utterly helpful.

- **Do not blame yourself for relapsing.** This could really happen. One moment you are OK, and the next thing you know you are back to your old habits. It is not OK, of course, but this does not necessarily mean that you have failed. Relapsing is a major possibility for eating disorders and is also a part of the entire recovery system, but blaming yourself for it would only worsen your condition. Remember that all efforts made for your recovery is already a part of the success. If you fall off the wagon this time, take the time to pick yourself up once again and hop on.

- **Keep educating yourself about pain management and healing techniques.** There is a plethora of studies going on these days and sooner or later, more breakthroughs will come knocking at your door. It is essential that you also take the time to read regularly, so if there is one specific medicine that would become available on the market, you can immediately consult your therapist about it. Having knowledge of the disease and its treatment is ultimately your main tool in breaking the eating disorder spell.

- **Get involved in the advocacy against physical and psychological pains.** If there is anyone who understands the complexity of the disorder, that would be YOU. Knowing the difficulties, the struggles, and a number of sacrifices people have made to help you combat such disorder should be encouraging enough for you to take part in helping other sufferers recover. There are many organizations and support groups that would also appreciate your personal involvement. Getting involved is both beneficial to others as well as to yourself.

- **Listen to the people who have completely healed and are now happy.** It is most certain that you are not alone in this battle. Some may have just gone ahead of you while others are still starting out. To continuously inspire you, listen to the real stories of survivors. Understand where they encounter the plot twist in their lives and how they countered it. We, as human beings, are designed to learn from one another. Do the same- take the time to listen and ponder on their experience later.

The journey may be long towards full recovery, and so it is vital that you hold on to it tight. Your thriving recovery will not only change the way you live but could also inspire a thousand others who are on the same boat. Celebrate life by healing completely.

Chapter 14 -- Healing The Mind And Body With Natural Supplements

Taking the route to natural treatment and approach is still seen as the better way of resolving health problems and promoting healing of the body and the mind. At present, many people are becoming more and more keen on taking supplements to boost their health. The effects of these supplements can be best achieved when taken with caution, regular exercise, healthy food choices, and well-managed stress levels.

Here are the top supplements that are excellent in supporting healing of the body and mind.

1. Combined Chondroitin and Glocosamine

According to a research conducted by the US National Library of Medicine, both Chondroitin and Glucosamine are natural bodies compounds. The former can be extracted from the cartilage that surrounds the joints while the latter can befound in the fluids in the joints. The increased level of these compounds in the body has first been found effective in treating chronic knee problem. Pain management physicians have also started to also prescribe these supplements to people suffering from body pain problems. However, the dosage and the frequency of taking must be first identified by the health care practitioners.

2. Omega-3 Fatty Acids

The intake of omega-3 fatty acids has been practiced for a long time and has been mainly used in reducing inflammation. It is likewise a good supplement that promotes brain development. These can now be taken capsule form or be taken naturally by eating fish rich in these fatty acids such a salmon, tuna, sardines, and green leafy vegetables.

Although this particular supplement can help ease body pain, it should be taken with utmost care as it could have an adverse impact on people taking blood-thinning medication. A good dosage of omega-3 fatty acids can also help in the improvement of brain work.

3. Devil's Claw

This supplement comes from a herb called Harpagophytum procumbent that can only be found in native Africa. The extracts of this plant called harp ago side are used as the supplement and are produced as supplements, usually in 50-milligram tablets. These supplements are taken to cure lower back pain. The natural extracts from this African pain may drastically reduce inflammation. Devil's claw is becoming more and more common these days. It is important to verify the active ingredients in the supplement you are buying and make sure that harp ago side is one of them.

4. Capsaicin

Capsaicin has long been used an alternative medicine for centuries. This can be found in various variants of peppers. This is the agent that produces heat. Although most supplements come in capsule or tablet form, capsaicin is used by directly applying it as a cream. Cream with this heat-giving agent is normally applied directly onto the affected area around 4 times a day. There are also now patches that contain this active ingredient. The agent is used to desensitize the channels through which pain signalsare sent to the brain receptors.

Back in 2011, a study conducted alongside 1,500 respondents proved that capsaicin really helps in relieving pain. The result of the study was published in the Journal of Pain Research. The result also shows that people that endure musculoskeletal pain may feel a long-term relief of up to eight weeks when capsaicin is used properly.

5. Turmeric

Due to its strong and proven anti-inflammatory properties, turmeric is also one of the frequently prescribed supplements for people with chronic back pain issues. This is the spice more commonly found in curry dishes. More importantly, this is a spice that taken due to its medicinal properties.Tumeric supplement can be taken in capsule form, as a liquid extract, or as a tea mixture. Although this is generally safe for the consumption of the adults, doctors also warn that people may gallbladder disease should not use it for medication.

6. Vitamin D

Vitamin D is essential in making your bones and teeth strong.Sufficient intake of Vitamin D can also be used to manage back problems such as lumbar spinal stenosis. The regular intake of Vitamin D can also prevent the development of osteoporosis, particularly for people 40 years old and above. Peopleare advised taking at least 15 micrograms of Vitamin Do a daily basis. However, the dosage you may need depends on the finding of your doctors. Aside from obtaining Vitamin D from milk and dairy products, doctors also recommend early morning sunlight exposure.

Apart from Vitamin D, there are also vitamins and minerals that can help maintain strong backbone and help resist injury or pain. See the next chapter and get educated about the benefits of the vitamins.

7. Vitamin A

This vitamin is an important antioxidant that shields your body from certain diseases. As an antioxidant, it helps rebuild the damaged tissues by promoting healthy cell production. This is helpful in the formation of the bone and the efficient use of protein in the body. Vitamin A can be found in dairy products, eggs, chicken liver, spinach, sweet potato, oranges, nectarines, and carrots.

8. Vitamin B12 (Vitamin B Complex)

This vitamin promotes the production of healthy bone marrow. It also helps in the normal functioning and growth of the spine. Vitamin B can be taken as a supplement or can be found in food such as red meat, fish, chicken, yogurt, cheese, liver, and eggs.

9. Vitamin C

This is an important vitamin that promotes healing. It is a

catalyst for collagen production that helps cells transform tissues. Said collagenic effect is essential in repairing ligaments and tendons that are injured over wear-and-tear. Vitamin C also helps in keeping the tissues of the vertebral discs and ligaments strong. Common sources of Vitamin C include sweet potatoes, strawberries, citrus fruits, kiwi, tomatoes, broccoli, green peppers, spinach and yam.

10. Vitamin K

This vitamin is essential for the proper usage of calcium in the body. Calcium is better absorbed by the bones and teeth with the presence of Vitamin K. This can be found in broccoli, liver, pork, spinach, and different dairy products.

11. Calcium

This mineral is vital to maintaining a healthy level of bone mass, particularly during the old age. Bones may become brittle and weak when calcium intake become insufficient. Consequently, a brittle bone may result in painful fractures in the spine which may produce the long-term or chronic brain. To avoid this, one must take calcium supplements or obtain their calcium from sources like salmon, sardines, cheese, milk, yogurt, sesame seeds, black beans, almonds, brown sugar, and peanuts.

12. Iron

This mineral helps maintain healthy cells which deliver a good amount of oxygen to every part of the body. It also helps the body produce sufficient myoglobin which is an essential muscular component that mainly functions as a support to the spine. Iron supplements are now readily available on the market. However, natural sources of iron can also be obtained from beans, eggs, soy, lentils, grains, kale, broccoli, and spinach.

13. Magnesium

 This mineral helps promote better contraction and relaxation of muscles. It also helps in keeping the muscles toned and the bones dense enough. Having sufficient magnesium also promotes the healthy usage of proteins in the body. Sources of magnesium include beans, bananas, seeds, grains, nuts, avocados, shrimps, kiwi, kale, broccoli, and spinach.

Understanding how these supplements work in the body can boost your health as well as promote swift healing.

Chapter 15 - Healing The Most Common Physical Pain

Back pain is one of the common health problems. In fact, it is too common that 80% of the entire population in the US experience this kind of pain at least once in their whole life. Sufferers of back pain may be as young as 20 years or as old as 90. Moreover, back problems are much more common to middle-aged men and women.

As the back is also a complex part of the body, the pain in the area may be linked to various organs such as the vertebrae discs, the spinal cord, the nerves, the bony lumbar spine, the abdomen, the lower back muscles, and the internal organs within the pelvic area. Although less common, pain in the upper part of the back may also be experienced by people suffering from tumors within the chest area, spinal inflammation, and aorta disorders.

Lower back pain may stem from various causes including lifting, being seated for a long time, or a sudden movement. Lower back pain can also be triggered by bending forward or backward. It is important to remember to see a doctor right away if severe back pain is felt when coughing or sneezing, or when the back pain is accompanied by leg pain, numbness, and sore in within the hip area.

Back problems are not always simple. In fact, certain causes may not easily be determined immediately even by health practitioners. However, it is still best to consult a doctor before trying out any home remedies. Experiencing lower back problem may only be secondary to another medical condition. This is why long-term treatment is sometimes needed.

Here are the common red flags linked to spinal pain that you should watch out for:

- There is a throbbing or striking pain in the upper part of the spine/back (thoracic spine)
- The pain occurs regularly or consistently
- The pain occurs while taking steroidal drugs
- The pain happened after a road traffic accident
- You have had cancer or still being treated when the back pain started to occur
- There is an obvious weight loss
- The back pain is accompanied by numbness, bowel disturbance, abrupt weakness
- You suspect that there is deformity in your spine
- Your back pain is accompanied by recurring fever

If you happen to experience any of the red flags above, it is wise to set up an appointment with your doctor immediately. This to know whether what you are experiencing is just a common mechanical pain or not.

It is also essential to understand the different risk factors linked to back pain. These factors include the following: stressful job/ stressful environment

- Sedentary lifestyle
- Pregnancy
- Abrupt weight gain/obesity
- Smoking
- Vigorous physical activities
- The gender as women are more prone to back problems than men
- Age

You may be wondering as to why back part of the torso is so susceptible to pain and injuries. The reason behind this lies in the musculoskeletal system of the human body. The back region of the body is made up of a series of complex ligaments, bones, disks, tendons, muscles that are all connected via he presence of pads that look like cartilage. As this region is considered complex in structure,

Below are the most common reasons for experiencing back pain:

1. Daily activities

- Twisting
- Carrying heavy load
- Pushing rigorously
- Bending awkwardly
- Sleeping on the stomach
- Sleeping on a bad mattress/bed
- Stretching too much
- Long driving
- Poor sitting position
- Sitting on a low chair
- Sitting for a long period
- Standing for a long period

2. Strain

- Strained muscles
- Strained ligaments
- Muscle spasm

3. Structural pain

- Bulging discs
- Ruptured discs

- Regenerated discs

- Osteoporosis

- Spinal curvature

- Arthritis

- Sciatica

The following health practitioners can offer you the best treatment for the complete healing of your back problems:

1. An osteopath--This is a health practitioner whose approach generally involves visual and touching inspections. The method of osteopathy also includes rhythmic or slow stretching to check the patient's mobility level. An osteopath may also use pressure or other indirect manipulations to ease the pain in the joints or the muscles.

2. A physiotherapist or physical therapist --This is a health practitioner whose approach general involves the diagnosis and treatment of joint problems. A physical therapist is also trained to make sure that the soft tissues of the body are stress and pain-free.

3. A chiropractor --This is a health practitioner that will diagnose your back problem through visual inspection and palpation. One of the key approaches of a chiropractor is the use of spine alignment procedures. This is to make the appropriate adjustments on the spinal joints. Chiropractors also use scan results, imaging results, urine tests, and blood tests before performing any therapy.

Healing may require more than just the desire and will to achieve it. This is particularly true when it comes to getting rid of the most common physical pain - back pain. By keeping yourself educated and informed on how you can better care for your backs, you can be sure that you will not be needing to see any doctor soon. Now, you can obtain relevant information of back care by simple clicks on applications. In order to stave off the pain on your back, you can follow the guidelines and tips you can get using the following applications.

App #01: <u>Simplyhealth Back Care</u> -- This application offers up-to-date information and a wide range of advice of how to manage back pain effectively. It also contains easy-to-follow tips on how you prevent any form of back pain. One of the most interesting features of this app is the set of exercise videos you can do to strengthen your core and back muscles. There are also graphics that present a range of information on back care. Should you need a quick directory of healthcare practitioners near you are, all you have to do is to click on one of the buttons. This application also allows users to record information on their own experiences using the diary called 'Me and My Back'.

App #02: <u>The Back App</u> -- This is the app developed by renowned physical therapist Sarah Key. This app contains video tutorials on how you can deal with back problems efficiently. Moreover, information on back related issues can easily be watched using the series of videos you can access with a single tap.

App #03: <u>The Bad Back App</u> -- This application can help people with back problems by reminding them not to sit for a long period of time. It functions as an alarm to remind your to get on your feet and do a bit stretching or walk for a few minutes. This app works on vibration mode so it can immediately catch your attention.

App #04: <u>The BackDoctor App</u> -- This application offers an essential and practical guide that you can follow to prevent or reduce neck and lower back pain. The app features a series of easy-to-follow exercises that you can do anytime, anywhere. Each video is accompanied by explanatory photos and text in order to make the users understand the use and the results expected from performing them. The app features 5 different training programs that aim to strengthen the core and trunk muscles. The programs can all be performed even without having to go to the gym. Using this app, you can also keep track of the programs you have completed.

App #05: <u>The Back Pain Nerve Chart App</u> -- This is an app that can be used by both patients and chiropractors. The app features graphics with clear and easy-t-grasp spine diagrams which can help you find out the causes of your back problems.

Chapter 16 – Self-Healing Through Self-Hypnosis

What are the desires of your heart? Do you want to heal completely?

What do you want to achieve for yourself?

It may only take you a minute or two to ponder on these questions. But inevitably, you will be able to give at least one answer or two – and sometimes MORE.

People live in a realm inundated with dreams and goals of different sizes and magnitude. One of the most important desires that anyone can have is to undergo complete healing. Your personal desires may be different from others and so are your own means of achieving them. Some strive really hard just to get to the first step while others exert very little effort causing them to fail altogether. You do not need to be the latter as you already possess the very tool needed to turn every inch of your dream into a reality. You have Y-O-U!

By having YOU means you are able to perform SELF HYPNOSIS. Many people get the false idea about, but the bottom line is that this is a tool that benefits your entire being. It is a tool that opens doors to success. It is an instrument that allows you to break free from all the anxieties, fear, and unnecessary stress you have been languishing with. In short, you've got nothing to lose, but SO MUCH MORE to gain. Read on to understand the benefits of this tool to success.

It gives you a positive outlook

Self- hypnosis is no magic trick, BUT it can result in a lot of positivity. It changes your overall outlook in life. In this age where media platforms are filled with news on terrorism, political instability, calamities, hatred, WE all need some sprinkles of positivity in our lives. The problem also escalates when people tend to look for optimism in the wrong way. This is because many people have already forgotten how to become positive – how to truly interpret the diminishing line between optimism and realism.

Don't you envy kids sometimes? They can run around all day with bearing those huge smiles on their faces without any care in the world. Sadly, people have forgotten how to be like them, how to feel like them, how to isolate themselves from the ruthless truth about life. Going back to the basic is necessary. Reawaking the inner child in you is necessary to evoke more optimism. This is highly achievable with self-hypnotism. The moment you close your eyes, you start to step beyond the horizon of stress and pain, and you start to create a new pattern of positive thoughts. This then forces you to bring forth new set of habits that are free from negativity.

Keeps you enthusiastic

As self-hypnotism lets you achieve the inner 'wants' of your heart by envisioning them, it also builds a fountain of enthusiasm deep within your soul. Every session is a whole new experience. You get more and more excited each time you start performing it. And soon, you will see some real changes in your life.

The way you imagine your life is always at the best, at the happiest scenario. When you think about the goodness of your existence, you look at it with vibrant colors and you orchestrate every move as though directing the movie of your life. The excitement that builds deep inside you certainly pumps up more energy and enthusiasm. The power that exudes from your thoughts allows you do more and achieve more. With great enthusiasm, anything is achievable. Your face, your gesture, and your entire aura will soon let others know that there is something great happening to you – and the secret is something that you can just keep to yourself. Let them discover the truth by themselves.

Makes you energetic

As a great future awaits you, you can continue creating the steps towards it by self-hypnotism. You would embrace it soon with and through great energy. Positive thoughts are regarded as dominant magnets that attract positive energy. This then will bridge you to the things that you have always wanted – a good life, happiness, contentment – name it, and it will become YOURS. You will be able to develop your personal source of unceasing energy with the use of self-hypnotism. You need not live in the dark anymore. Cast the negative energy aside to give more space to positive energy.

Challenges you to be inventive

One of the secret to real happiness and success is just within your reach. Your mind has the power to change things. It does not have to go with the flow. If you aim for real results, you need to take on some diverse steps. You can do this by being inventive – imaginative and creative. Your future does not necessary have to follow the standards. You can change the way you live – by creating the life that you want. And yes, it is as simple as it sounds.

Self-hypnotism allows you to become the successful lawyer that you want, the rich entrepreneur that you have been dreaming of, or the pilot that you once aimed for. The opportunities and choices are infinite. Your life does not have to be solely based on your environment – it has to be foremost controlled by YOU through your thoughts. Never ever put a limit on yourself because just like the prominent figures you know, YOU are also built for greatness!

Sparks your drive to succeed

Have you ever wanted something so badly that it leaves a gnarl on your face when you think about it? That is the so-called 'drive' working on you. And that drive springs because of a certain goal. This is exactly why self-hypnotism is your best tool for achieving the elusive success. It gives you the opportunity to be on fire all the time. It feels as though you are ready step on the gas to seize an opportunity. So why stop?

People fail because they are not driven enough. The fire starts to get extinguished when your motivational tank is not constantly refilled. Never let this happen. Keep your fire burning until you reach to a scorching level of success. Nothing else and no one else will take you there. It will always be just YOU and your dream working hand-in-hand.

Chapter 17- Healing Your Mind From 'Tech' Overload

In this chapter you will learn how completely heal from your technology and information overload. In present world of electronic media communication, the social media like Facebook, twitter, what's apps, YouTube, Pinterest, etc. are being very popular to people all through the world. Billions of users use these media in their everyday life and a huge number new users are also being created daily. So, there are a lot of information overload in these social media, which is a big problem now.

Comparatively what's apps is less overloaded than Facebook, Twitter, YouTube, Pinterest and other social media because, in what's apps, there are some limited use like writing video chatting, audio call, texting, etc. So, you can control and limit your use here. On the other hand, Facebook, Twitter, YouTube and other social media users are suffering from information overload because of their architectural structure and lot of features. Now, the question is how to overcome the information overload from these media? Here are some steps by which we can lessen our information overload from these types of social communication media.

1. Limit your friend list: There are a lot of persons who are using Facebook, Twitter, YouTube, Pinterest and other social communication media. Some people are intended to increase the friend list unnecessarily to collect many likes on their posts. Therefore, you may get many friend requests every day. You need to be selective before adding them. Visit the profile before adding to your list and if you see that the profile is good for nothing, then just ignore. Don't add unnecessary friends to your list or don't follow to the persons who are using social communication media just to pass their time. Otherwise, your Newsfeed will be overloaded unnecessarily and you may overlook the information which was really needed for you.

2. Ignore unproductive group or pages: Especially in Facebook, you'll see that many people are adding you to their groups or requesting to like their pages which are really unproductive and has no use. Just leave these kinds of group and don't give like those pages. Otherwise, many unnecessary information you'll get in your profile everyday which will make you bothered and your time will be wasted. So, just add to such groups or pages which are productive and you'll be benefited from their information. Suppose, if you are a health professional, you may be added to the medical science related pages or groups which will help in your profession.

3. Follow local community: You can make a list of your local business, journalists, writers, etc. in your social communication media like Facebook and Twitter to get important and productive news from them.

4. Avoid unnecessary chatting: On Facebook, what's apps, etc., you'll see that many people are knocking you in chatting just to say hi, hello and will message just to pass time. If not necessary, just ignore these kinds of chatting and focus to productive information to make the best use of your time.

5. Follow authentic news media: In social communication media, you'll find many online news media, creating everyday who are providing many prone news and fake news just to make the people attracted to their community. Don't follow these types of news media otherwise you'll be overloaded with many fake and unproductive information through them. Follow only the authentic new media to get real information.

6. Unfollow them whom you cannot unfriend: Especially in Facebook, you'll get some friends who are everyday giving in their posts most unnecessary and unproductive information. If you think that your friend or relative may be hurt if you unfriend them, just unfollow. As a result you will not get their information or post in your timeline, but they'll still remain in your friend list.

7. Make list of real friends and family: In social communication media like Facebook and Twitter, we want to stay close to our real friends and family. Make a list of friends and family and response to their posts regularly. As a result, you'll get their information in your Facebook or Twitter as priority basis and this is the great way to separate them from others.

8. Use search tools to find out your necessary information: On YouTube, pinterest and these types of social media, use search tools and put your subject there so that you can easily find your necessary or related topic out of thousands of content. This will save your time and you'll not be puzzled to find out your information from many. You can take the help of Google or other search engines for this task.

Chapter 18 - Heal Your Mind By Changing Your Routine

Healing the mind is not only about getting rid of the pain and the malady. Changing the routine and being mindful of the environment you have also help in clearing your mind and cultivating a more positive thought.

Here are some tips given on how you can rebuild a healthier routine for your mind:

1. Keep sometimes for yourself in your daily routine: In spite of a huge load of information, you need to keep sometimes in your daily routine to spend with your family. Turn off all your information devices like TV, cell phone, computer, etc. and spend that time with your family, friends or with your closest one and relax.

2. Keep at least one day off weekly: Take at least one day off per week, keep your mind fresh and out of any kind of thinking on that day. Go outside with your friends and family and recharge yourself to work for the rest of the day of week.

3. Reduce the reading of unnecessary information: If you are using lots of sources for information and taking a huge information daily, then you need to reduce the amount of information to live optimally. All the information you are taking daily, is not necessary for you. So, don't focus yourself to unnecessary information and focus on your necessary information only.

4. Make a time schedule: You need to make a time schedule for every work. Make a time to check e-mail, Facebook, Pinterest, YouTube, etc. Keep selective time to read newspaper and to watch TV.

5. Limit your friends in social media network: You may have a lot of friends in your social media networks and you are getting overwhelmed with the feeds. So, cut off some of the friends from your list to whom you are not making any necessary communication.

6. Use your idle time: Sometimes we have to pass idle times sitting on bus in traffic jam, waiting in doctor's appointment, etc. You can use these idle times which will reduce the pressure on you later. You can bring your necessary book with you or bring a notepad and complete some of your works whatever you can in this idle time.

7. Turn off your mobile during important task: When you are doing some important task which needs a full concentration or when you are in an important meeting, some phone calls may interrupt your attention as well as others'. So, turn off your cell phone on that time. You may use miss call notification so that you can check the list who called you and can phone back later if necessary.

8. Don't make your number visible to all in a social network: In social networks, make your phone number visible to only you so that others cannot see it. Otherwise, your number will be spread to a lot of persons who may make unnecessary calls to you just to say hi hello or talking without any reason.

9. Move messages from inbox: If you need to deal with a lot of message everyday, move the messages after finishing the task. You can make subject-wise sub folders under inbox so that you can easily get them when needs to recheck. If you keep lots of message in your inbox, then you may be confused or can be focused to previous work which will interrupt your current work.

10. Finish your daily task properly: Whatever work you are doing, you need to finish your daily task properly. If necessary, give some extra time to your work to accomplish them. Otherwise, your mind will not be fresh which will affect your health and personal life.

11. Don't review any information at off work time: When are passing your time with your family, taking rest at your off time, don't think about what you did, what to do next day, what will be the effect of your today's work, etc. If do so, you are just spoiling your off time which might be more enjoyable with your family. This kind of think may peer to your mind, but you need to put them away because thinking on them will actually not bring any solution to your work.

Despite the fact that we have all been very much influenced by the changing environment and needs we naturally develop, it is still essential to remind ourselves that taking some time off would help eliminate the unnecessary junk our mind. By 'detoxifying', healing can take place more efficiently and effectively.

Chapter 19 - Embracing The Ancient Self-Healing Techniques

The best remedies for the pains of the mind, heart, and spirit brought about by such fast-paced existence may not always be what the president may bring us. Most of the time, going back to the basic or embracing the ancient healing techniques remain to be the most effective.

Anywhere across the globe, you can always find individuals who have not just become accustomed to the application of these ancient techniques of healing, but have made them the natural part of their lives. The immense, mind, body, and overall health benefits of these alternative approaches have also been a subject for researches which now make them science-supported.

Yoga, Pilates, and the growing popularity of meditation and mindfulness practices have likewise all been tried and tested by millions of people who are aiming at a healthier mind, body, and general well being. These methods can certainly work wonders without the having to take anything orally.

Here are examples of self-healing techniques you can always try:

1. Tai Chi

This has the same effect as yoga. Though it is basically a form of physical exercise, the benefit can be seen in the calming effect it can give you. Originally, Tai Chi was solely considered as a form of a Chinese Martial Art that aims to unlock the energy force called Qi. This practice requires intense focus on breathing, mindful movement, and attention.

Scientific studies have likewise revealed that the practice of Tai Chi, when combine with traditional Chinese medicine, can result in healthy bone density, reduction of pain, and improved conditions of breast cancer patients. Tai Chi also reduced hypertension and promotes heart health. Now, the Tai Chi and Mind-Body Research Program of the Harvard University is looking at it as a standard medical-type of treatment that can promote rehabilitation of conditions.

2. Reiki

Reiki is the one of the biggest contributions of Japan when it comes to self-healing. This form of art fundamentally expresses that healing can be accomplished through the power of touch. Reiki is generally performed by traditional practitioners by placing their hands on the body of the patient in order to stimulate and regulate the energy of life force.

Reiki has been found to be effective at reducing and even eliminating pain, stress, anxiety, depression, and fatigue. Over the years, Reiki healing has likewise become more popular in the US and many holistic care centers have incorporated this to their healing practices.

3. Reflexology

The application of pressure on certain points of the hands, body, and face has been the main tool of reflexology. Many ancient healing experts believe that that through body mapping, these pressure points get heal specific organs of the body.

Contrary to what many believe, reflexology is not just any form of massage. Although it can clearly promote relaxation and relief from stress and anxiety, this method has a much deeper healing effect. It can be performed in order to reduce depression and get rid of the pain as a whole.

4. Ayurveda

This centuries-old Indian healing practice has also started to become as popular as yoga and meditation in the US. The growing interest in this 'science of life' (as defined by Indians) has been attributed to the uniqueness of the formula that includes lifestyle, herbal supplements, and food in general. If Tai Chi is all about Qi, Ayurveda focuses on re-balancing these three energy types known as the pitta, vata, and kapha. Pitta is equivalent to the fire element of the Chinese and is responsible for the transformation. Vata is defined as the energy of the motion and is tantamount the Chinese element of air. Lastly, Kapha is the energy that promotes growth and is equivalent of the element called 'earth'.

In the Ayurvedic healing techniques, the disturbances that lose the balance of these energies are believed to manifest as a form of a disease. This may include unhealthy diet, stress, weather, and even personal relationships. The doshas (or the energy) have to be put in balance to regain health and promote healing.

Conclusion

Loving yourself is fundamental to achieving the quality of life you deserve. Your mind has so much power that you can harness in order to promote healing and overall health. There is so much you can do to improve your well being, as well as to cultivate that love for yourself that you truly deserve.

Healing your mind helps to heal your body. The two are important interlinked parts of you that need to run smoothly and in harmony. This book has shown you how the mind body connection works and how it can heal you and make you a much happier person. It is hoped that you have gleaned sufficient information to get your life back on track because that's the intention.

When you have this extraordinary gift of self-healing, you want to shout it from the rooftops. I remember sitting on that hill one night and thinking how fortunate I am to have experienced the healing power of the mind. Once you heal the mind, the body will take care of itself, as the mind controls the processes that happen to make you feel complete and whole, even if you experience illness.

Go forward in your life and learn humility and learn that healing comes from all of the powerful positive aspects of what you think. If you think in a negative manner, your life becomes that negative place because you block the healing of the body. Once you learn to step beyond that, you will indeed find yourself in a place of peace where healing happens without any intervention from you. That's when you know you have self-belief, hope and happiness awaiting you for the rest of your life. That's when you also embrace life and love the life that you have been given.

RECOMMENDED READING

HEALING: Heal Your Body Heal Your Life

smarturl.it/healingaa

CRYSTAL HEALING ENERGY

smarturl.it/crystala

SELF ESTEEM: Confidence Building: Overcome Fear, Stress and Anxiety: Self Help Guide

hyperurl.co/selfesteem

Boundaries: Line Between Right And Wrong
hyperurl.co/boundaries

Anger: Natural Treatments To Manage Frustration And Stress

hyperurl.co/anger

HEARING GOD'S VOICE: How To Hear The Voice Of God

smarturl.it/heargod

Printed in Great Britain
by Amazon